CONTENTS

CHAPTER ONE
INTRODUCTION

WHAT IS LIFE?

Without life the earth will be meaningless, Life is therefore, the ability of any living thing to function and grow or the existence of an individual or living thing and their activities. We can see that in the beginning, God created the heavens and the earth, but the earth was formless and empty, darkness was over the surface of deep (Gen 1v1-2a). So in the beginning, all things were made by God. He started from the moment of creation and moved forward to the creation of humanity. John 1v1. It is after the creation of human beings that other activities started to unfold, God ordered man to name other creatures, then man named all animals and living creatures. So life then became interesting, meaningful, and full of activities. People started to function and grow. People began to struggle for survival, gave birth to children, train them to mention but a few. All these began after the disobedience of man to God, and man was driven out of the Garden of Eden.

So you can agree with me that life is full of challenges and mistakes. These challenges need to be faced and surmounted, by articulating and achieving positive and feasible goals. If one fails to plan one plans to fail. Life is the best school while God is the best teacher, problem is the best assignment and failure, the best revision. You should, therefore, be the best you can in life. If you do not imbibe the secrets of life achievements, you will face the consequences emanating or resulting from the ignorance of the secrets of life achievements which is destiny failure or unattained destiny.

Life is a stage. This means there are categories of life existence, but I will like us to deliberate on the stages below:

❖ Spiritual life

❖ Physical life

❖ Educational life

❖ Youthful life

❖ Marital life

SPIRITUAL LIFE

Spiritual life is the most vital aspect of life without which one will be hopeless and dead though one may still be physically alive.

The bible says "what shall it profit a man if he gains the whole world and loses his own soul" Luke 9vs 25.

Again, what God has prepared for his people, I mean those who are faithful to the end is eternal life. It is also written "the eye has not seen nor ear heard nor has it entered the heart of man the things which God has prepared for those who love Him 1Corithian 2v9. Furthermore, the spiritual life controls all other aspects of life. With spiritual life, we interact with our maker, the Almighty God. For we are spirit just as God is.

PHYSICAL LIFE.

Physical life is associated with the on going life. This aspect of life is very important, because any mistake made may lead to perpetual frustration in life. Such mistakes may be living a wayward life such as fornication, committing abortion killing and engaging in other evil acts. These may, in turn result in childlessness in life, contracting sexually transmitted diseases such as, HIV and AIDS. Bad behaviours may result in a person, remaining single for life. There is an adage that says that respect is reciprocal, and that what you garbage in will be garbage out. Good and bad deeds have their rewards. Before you finish reading this book, you will be able to know the secrets of life achievement and apply it to day to day activities. It will lead you to have positive destiny achievement.

EDUCATIONL LIFE.

This is the life lived during the period of your educational life. Tell me your friend and I will tell you who you are. Remember that education without good manners is vanity. Never you cheat because a cheat must be cheated. Work hard, don't play away your time because time is precious and once missed will never come back again.

- Don't join the multitude to do evil
- Bridle your tongue because death and life are in the power of the tongue
- Don't hate any of your teachers or lecturers.
- Study ahead of your teacher so that you can ask questions after teaching and it will make you understand better.
- Be focused in life because that determines your success or failure in life.

- Fear God, because the fear of God is the beginning of wisdom.

YOUTHFUL LIFE.

Youthful life is the prime of life full of the exciting exuberance. At this stage of life, youths find themselves at the crossroad and face certain challenging experiences that tend to draw them away from the purpose of God. Those challenges may come from the society, peer group, love of money and parental upbringing.

These challenges mentioned above are interwoven. There is need for good parental child upbringing. The bible says in proverb. 22v16, train up a child in the way he should go, and when he is old he will not depart from it. This is very important because it is the foundation of child training that facilitates child behaviours.

When children are moulded with the word of God, the fear of God will automatically be in built in them, They will be wiser than their colleagues. No wonder, the bible says, "The fear of God is the beginning of wisdom". So, a child should be taught the ordinances of God and His faithfulness, to obey God in all ramifications and to avoid sins of all kinds. They should also be taught that the wages of sin is death. Parents must also play very vital roles in the lives of their children, so that they will be role models to other children. This will make the training of these children fruitful. Believe me, these children will never be influenced by the society, or peer group because they have hidden the word of God in their heart so that they will not sin against God Ps 119v11 vice versa.

In the area of love of money, they have known what God says about "love of money" in the word of God, 1st Tim 6 v10. "The love of money is the root of all evils." So, because of the training and knowledge concerning what God says about the love of money; they will run for their dear lives. Child training and upbringing play vital roles in the lives of the youth who are potential leaders. Though, according to Arinze (1980) and Nworie (2002), "it is true that a good child does not always emerge logically from good parents" but after parents have genuinely done their inculcation of good training in their children, the chances of bad children emerging from them are quite limited if not totally zero.

Finally, Hughes (2010) indicated that children from divorced families or broken families are more likely to have academic problems, to be aggressive and get in trouble with school authorities or the police, have low self esteem and feeling of depression, have difficulties, getting along with their siblings, peers and their parents. In adolescence they are more likely to engage in diligent activities, to get involved in sexual activities and experiment with illegal drugs. In adolescence and in young adult hood, they are more likely to have some difficulties, forming intimate relationships and establishing independence from their families.

MARITAL LIFE.

Marriage is an institution ordained by God Himself at the Garden of Eden. When God saw the loneliness of man, He gave him a "helpmate" a rib from man was used to make a woman by God "Gen 2v22". Therefore, shall a man leave his father and mother and be joined to his wife, and they shall become one flesh "Gen 2v24" from that union the marital life begins. Marital life needs to be handled very carefully because it is very delicate in the sense that if not handled well, it may lead to divorce which is against God's will. If it is handled well, it will lead to enjoying heaven on earth, where peace and harmony reign. According to Nworie "2002" "God does not only will that there should be family, but more importantly, he wills that these families, should be in peace without which they will be like proliferating little hells on earth" "The family is the basic unit of the society and consists of those individuals, male or female, youth or adult, legally related, genetically or not genetically. Barman, Snyder, koshered Erg (2008).

Further more, every body mentioned or involved in family will be taken care of by the husband and wife (Home managers). Every body should accord the respect due to one another, both young and old, so that peace will reign supreme in a family. The children and the youth need serious training both physically, spiritually, educationally or otherwise because they are potential leaders. When a foundation is faulty, evil will reign in our society. Righteousness exalts a nation, but sin is a reproach to any nation. So, let all hands be on deck for better tomorrow. Hence, here are some of the essential ingredients or secrets of success.

- Get on well with people
- Try to understand others better
- Try to be yourself
- Be cautions
- Avoid being an imitator of your fellow humans
- Be respectful because it is reciprocal
- Avoid Gossips
- Be content with what you have
- Avoid too much talking
- Trust fully in God and in the strength of His might
- Walk and talk gracefully because you are an embodiment of grace.

We are advised not only to read this book, but to put in practice what we have learnt. Keep on reading, for more lessons will still be exposed.

CHAPTER TWO
CHALLENGES OF LIFE

All of us face both minor and major challenges in our lives. How we deal with those life challenges determine how we are experienced in life. We struggle to survive. Overcoming life challenges is a serious issue. It offers the insights needed to master the secrets of life achievements. Through this mastery, the joy of ordinary day to day existence culminates in the refined wine of success and joy in life. This is one of the challenges that was positively achieved by Mary's faith in Jesus as she has mastered Jesus and knew what He could do.

Why must we be challenged?

Every single day, we are faced with some life challenges. Some times, the challenges defeat us and we suffer, sometimes we are victorious, and from our experiences, we learn and grow. Surprisingly, all life challenges are initiated by the soul. Though it can appear that our problems come from other people, society and circumstances. In fact, they arise to support our personal growth in consciousness http//www.soul-books.com/life-challenge 2011. Every challenge is something in the form of energy or quality trying to become a part of our consciousness. Because we are not yet familiar with this energy, we have to learn what it is and how to incorporate it in to our lives. When it is incorporated, this produces transformation (Jane 2010). Some lesser quality, such as selfishness, has given way to some greater quality, such as love. We must face challenges because it paves way for greater achievements.

Master some life's major challenges

All of our challenges have a direct relationship to our soul's purpose in life. Our soul's purpose can be seen as having some aspects or dimensions of living. As souls, we try to manifest our energy fully in some ways or directions. When we master these, we are totally successful and have fulfilled our purpose perfectly.

Though, we each, has a unique purpose, the areas of challenges in life are common to us all. This book explores some major challenges we all face in order to fulfill the purpose for which we have come into this life. And it offers the keys and insight needed to master each essential aspect of our soul's purpose. With this new understanding, we can begin to welcome the challenges we meet. We will know how to learn from those challenges. And we will delight in using our new knowledge to love and serve the needs around us. Are you ready for new understanding of life challenges? When we resist the influence of the soul within, we:-

- Become ill

- Suffer accidents and injuries

- Become unhappy

- Have money problems

- Experience emotional pains

- Struggle with relationships

- Depression and despair may set in.

- Desire to live an expensive life style

Alchemy(Jane 2010)

Furthermore, we must face life as it is. Don't say "if things were different I would have done something" Do something with them as they are. Facing your life as it is now and winning is the objective. When things become hard and money stops flowing in, or you lose your Job and everything goes wrong, take stock of your life. Check what is wrong. See what you have forgotten and go on to conquer. We dream what we would do if Kenyon (2010) now wipes out the "if" Dream, and do it regardless of circumstance. Everything can be done. It depends on the man who wills to do it, who puts up the fight, and is willing to do the work.

The problem with people is that they want to get it too easily. We take our failures to be as a result of lack of opportunities. Therefore, we should fight until opportunities come. Success, belongs to the man who simply wills to get it. He is the man who makes success come his way. The fellow who lies down saying, "I can't do it" is a failure. Never lose hope because the first efforts failed. Go back and find the reason. Pick up the wreckage of old failures and build them into success.

You can succeed. I did not believe this before. I thought that there were but a few who had real ability, and that the rest of us belonged to the weak. I venture to say that it will be almost impossible to pick out a single person in any large establishment who does not have the ability in him that could make him outstanding, if it were developed. I am revealing this secret to the ambitious man or woman and not for the man who is too lazy to develop what is in him but for the man who is unsatisfied with anything, but the best.

As I study men and women, I am convinced of this: There are very few who have developed to limit the possibilities in them. There is no over development. Many people are in the wrong place in life. They have no talent for the things they are trying to do.

They are doing it simply to get by. There is enough salary waiting for the man who has the ability and is willing to put hard work into it. Choose your work, rather than have the work in which you have no interest. Find out what you can do, what you like best to do I don't care what your handicap is. There is never a handicap that could hold any man down who had in him the yeast to rise. Most of the people who are at the bottom are at the bottom, of the pit because they like to stay there. That is where they belong. It is a hard thing to say, but it is true. I am now what I wanted through Christ who prospers and strengthens me all these years. The first thing to do is to find out what you want. Set your eyes on the goal. Then fight for it. There must be an objective. When you find that objective, set your compass and sail for that star "Kenyon 2010"

More importantly, using what is in you have a long way to go to achieve your objective. There is a gold mine hidden in every life. Nature never made any failure or mistake. Every man has success hidden away in his soul. No one else can find it but himself. He holds the key to the hidden treasure. Failure comes because we tried to find it somewhere else. You can't find it anywhere else. Success, victory, achievement are in you. The exceptional people are those who develop what is in them.

Geniuses have grown up to weed for it, just because they developed the things they have via hard work. You will learn to love hard work. There are no great gold nuggets lying on top of the earth now. You have to go down into the earth for them. You must dig for them.

You want the applause of the work. You want money to buy clothes and build splendid houses? Awake young men. Go and find that hidden place in your own life. Dig until you conquer.

CHAPTER THREE
MISTAKES OF LIFE

Mistakes are a part of being human. Appreciate your mistakes. They are: precious life lessons that can only be learnt the hard way. When it is a fatal mistake which, at least, others can learn from "AL Franken 2010"

Mistakes in life involve sharing personal mistake/short stories, funny, useful and educational ones ranging from love to disappointment. As this book is going on to narrate certain mistakes of life, just don't make fun of it but learn from mistakes of others so that you will not be a victim in the future. "Great services are not cancelled by one act or by one single error" (Alvin Toffen 2010).

Some of the mistakes of life depend on child upbringing, peer group influence, challenges of life like financial achievement, social status, Ego, self esteem and self Actualization.

In the area of child upbringing, a child trained in the fear of God with good Christian background must stand out. If the child imbibes the Christian teachings and grow by them and by the fear God in all his/her acts, he/she will rarely make mistakes in life. Note that, not all children that are brought up in the Christian way fear God. That's why I stress on the phrase "Fear of God". You cannot compare those children born from harlots untrained, and broken homes, roaming the streets, to those that have the fear of God in them. What of parents who use their children to make money through prostitution? You cannot blame the child because when he grows up, he will embrace prostitution as a way of life. There is one man living in the Southern part of Nigeria. For the fact that he grew up there and the people he associated with were womanizers, he became a lecher too. He didn't find anything wrong in fornication because it is their way of life. It is only when he came back to his hometown that he repented. He approached a lady for friendship. The lady in turn preached to the young man about the dangers of friendship with the opposite sex. This may lead to lust of the flesh, fornication, an unwanted pregnancy, abortion or murder of the only available child a girl/lady may have in her life time. This is a very serious mistake in life and also sin against God. Let us, therefore be cautious in all our dealings.

Further more, the lady preached Christ and repentance to the young man. To the glory of God, the boy accepted Christ and, repented genuinely. He confessed to the lady that he could not before sleep without a woman. So my readers, please let us train our children in the fear of God. When we see the youth misbehaving, let us call them to order so that they will not go astray or make mistakes in life. "He who wins souls is wise".

More importantly, mind the environment in which you train your children and the type of friends they associate with. All things being equal if all these things were into consideration, our children will not make mistakes in life. Everybody wants to make it in life. That is why there is financial squabble here and there. Everybody wants to make it by all means, be it by stealing, kidnapping, entering into cultism at school, or occult group in adults, not minding whether it pleases God or not. Everybody wants to build a magnificent houses, estates, ride expensive cars, forgetting that we are all strangers in this world. All these possessions will be left behind when death strikes. Why not fear God, because His fear is the beginning of wisdom. Hear this story: A rich man that was riding the costliest reigning Jeep in town came to a filling station to purchase fuel. One of his classmates saw him and rushed to him, hoping to collect money from him, since he was a poor labourer. After exchanging pleasantries, the Labourer said to him, I wish I were you. The man rebuked him seriously and told him not to say that because he had made a great mistake in life by joining an occult group and had used parts of his body for sacrifice. He confessed that the area was full of dead tissues and that very offensive odour oozed out of it. He always used perfume to reduce the offensive odour and that the time of his death was fast approaching. At night, he would change to a dog and ate rubbish in the dustbins or refuse dump. He didn't even have any wife, let alone children, he narrated. He wanted to start afresh, but he had no opportunity again. So after narrating his life story to that poor labourer, his classmate, the labourer didn't know when he drew back to his place of work and pitied the rich man. So, don't envy anybody but just be yourself, and strive to make it. This is the only success that will last and you will live long with your family.

Further more, people make mistakes in pursuit of social status. They want to be known by all, have fame, ego, even self-esteem. When you are longing to have all these things so that you will assume self-actualization here on earth, it may influence you to engage in abnormal behaviours that are not pleasing to God. This may be going to native doctors to prepare you charm for protection and fame. Some even engage in witch craft, so that they will influence their opponents, just for fame sake.

Moreover, some of our students, in secondary and tertiary institutions want to make it fast. They engage in examination malpractices and certificate forgery. Some even buy results/certificates. These things profit them nothing. Some have ended up being drop outs in life. I know one boy at school who engaged in exam malpractices while he was at school. Unfortunately for him, he was caught in the act. The National Examination body banned him from taking any West African or NECO exams. The boy is now a drop out, an "Agboro at garage" What a grievous mistake of life. If he had bent down to read and face his examination without malpractice; he would have been somebody in life.

Dear readers, don't commit suicide, join armed robbers, or "419" fraudsters, cheats, embezzlers, rapists to mention a few. They are deviants who should be shunned. Wait on God, for your best days are still ahead. A patient dog eats the fattest bone. Look to Jesus the author and finisher of our faith. Our God will perfect all that concern us. Again, the thought God, our creator has for us is the thought of good, not of evil, to give us the desires of our hearts. Join us to say " NO" or shun evil, thereby, avoiding mistakes of life.

CHAPTER FOUR
GOALS AND STEPS OF LIFE ACHIEVEMENTS

WHAT IS GOAL?

Goal is something that you hope to achieve or to pursue e.g. achieve a goal. Sally (6th Edition). Furthermore, the company or individual can set some long-term and short-term organizational and personal goals.

Goal can also be described or illustrated using the mnemomic, GOALS which means:

G   –   Gather Facts

O   –   Organize a plan

A   –   Act on the plan

L   –   Look back and Review

S   –   Select new commitments

In goal setting, useful information and facts that can make impact on proposed plans should be gathered. After gathering all the facts, they are then organized into a plan. If the plan made is ignored, it becomes meaningless. So the plan must be acted on, to produce result. That means your goal has been achieved. Note that not all goals set will be achieved successfully. Some may back fire. Any outcome you see, be it good or bad should not discourage you. Review your plan and start a fresh.

More importantly, goals achieved should be maintained so that the products will be ever selling without any set back.

New products should be selected at intervals. This will help to promote the business and kills monotony, as we know that monotony kills interest.

The process of goal-setting helps you to choose where to go in life. By knowing precisely what you want to know, Plan to live your life. Mind tools, com/page 6.html Personal goal settings (2010). Many people feel as if they're adrift in the world.

They work hard, but they don't seem to get anywhere worthwhile. A key reason why they feel this way is that they haven't spent enough time to think out what they want in life, and haven't set for themselves formal goals. After all, would you set out on a major journey with no real idea of your destination, certainly not?

How to set powerful goals

Goal-setting is a powerful process for thinking about your ideal future and for motivating yourself to turn your vision of this your future into reality. The process of setting goals helps you to choose where you want to go in life. By knowing precisely what you want to achieve, you know where you have to concentrate your efforts on. You will also quickly spot the distractions, that can, so easily, lead you astray.

Why Set Goals?

Goal-setting is set by top-level Athlets, successful business people and achievers in all fields. Setting goals gives you long term vision and short term motivation. It focuses your acquisition of knowledge, and helps you to organize your time and your resources so that you can make the very best of your life. By setting defined goals, you can measure and take pride in the achievement of those goals and you will see forward progress in what might previously have seemed a long pointless objective. You will also raise your self-confidence, as you recognize your own ability and competence in achieving the goals that you have set.

Starting to set personal goals

You set your goals on a number of levels.

First you create your, "big picture" of what you want to do with your life (or over, say, the next 10 years and identify the large-scale goals that you want to achieve). Then, you break these down to smaller targets that you must hit to reach your lifetime goals. Finally, you have to plan, and start working on them to achieve these goals.

This is why we start the process of goal setting by looking at your lifetime goals. Then we work down to the things that you can do, say in the next five years then next year, next month, next week and today, to start moving, towards them.

Step 1: setting life time goals.

The first step in setting personal goals is to consider what you want to achieve in your lifetime. (Or at least, by a significant and distant time in the future). Setting lifetime goals gives you the overall perspective that surpasses all other aspects of your decision making.

To give a broad balance coverage of all importance ones in your life, try to set goals in some of the following categories (or in other categories of your own, where these are important to you).

Career:- What level do you want to reach in your career or what do you want to achieve?.

Financial:- How much do you want to earn ,by what stage? How is this related to your career goals?

Education:- is there any knowledge you want to acquire in particular? What information and skill will you need to have in order to achieve other goals?

Family:- Do you want to be a parent ? if so, how are you preparing to be a good parent? How do you want to be seen by a partner or members of your extended family?

Artistic: - Do you want to achieve any artistic goal?

Attitude: - is any part of your mindset holding you back? Is there any part of the way that you behave that upset you? (if so, set a goal to improve on your behaviour, or find a solution to the problem).

Physical: - Are there any athletic goals that you want to achieve, or do you want good health up to old age? What steps are you going to take to achieve this?

Pleasure: - How do you want to enjoy yourself?

Public service: - do you want to make the world a better place? If so how?

Brain storming: Select one or more goals in each category that best reflects on what you want to do. Consider breaking down again so that you will have a small number of really significant goals that you can focus on. As you do this, make sure that the goals that you have set are the ones that you genuinely want to achieve, not ones that your parent, family, or employers might want. Make sure you are not pliable. In short, be yourself.

Step 2:   Setting smaller goals

Once you have set your life time goals, set a five years plan of smaller goals that you need to complete if you are to reach your lifetime plan.

Then create a one-year plan, six-months plan, and a one month plan of progressively smaller goals that you should reach to achieve your lifetime goals

Each of these should be based on the previous plan. Then create a daily list of things that you should do today, to work toward your life time goals.

At early stage, your smaller goals might be to read books and gather information on the achievement of your higher levels goals. This will help you to improve on the quality and realism of your goal setting.

Finally review your plans, and make sure that they fit into the way in which you want to live your life.

Tips: if you feel that you are not paying attention to certain areas of your life, once you have decided on your first set of goals, keep the process going by reviewing and updating your to do list on a daily basis. Periodically review longer term plans and modify them to reflect your changing priorities and experiences (a good way of doing this is to schedule regular, repeating reviews using a computer based diary)

A useful way of making goals more powerful is to use the smart   mnemonic, SMART which usually stands for

S   Specific or significant

M   Measurable or meaningful

A   Achievable or action oriented

R   Relevant or rewarding

T   Time bound or tractable

For example, instead of having "to sail around the world" as a goal, it is more powerful to said "to have completed my trip around the world by Dec. 31 2015. It can be attainable if a lot of preparation work has been completed before. Hard goals can also be set as below:

1.	Be precise: Set precise goals, putting in dates time and amount so that it can measure achievements. If done like that, you will know when you have achieved the goals and have satisfaction after achieving them.

2.	Set priorities: when you have several goals give each a priority. This will help you to avoid sentiment on any other goals listed and direct you to the most important ones.

3.	Write goals down: This crystallizes them and gives them more force.

4.	Keep operational goals small: keep the low-level goals that you're working towards an achievement. If it is too large, it seems you are not making progress towards it.

5.   Set performance goal: not outcome goals. Set up goals that you should take care of have much control as possible.

6.   Set realistic goals: it is important to set goals that you can achieve (mind tools on goal setting) hppt.Mindtool.com. Be wise and make use of how to set goals and achieve them.

WHAT ARE ACHIEVEMENTS?

Achievements are the things that somebody has done successfully, especially using his own effort or skills. "Achievements come to someone by effort or skill from himself. Success comes when he empowers followers to do great things with him. Significance comes when he develops leaders to do great things for him. But a legacy is created when a person put his organization into

position to do great things without him" from
John C Maxwell.

CHAPTER FIVE
CONSEQUENCES, FOLLOWING IGNORANCE OF THE SECRETS OF LIFE ACHIEVEMENTS

The consequence means the effect or result of an action. All along, we have been deliberating on secrets of life achievements and on what you ought to do in order to be successful in life. There are three stages of human life, childhood, adolescence and adult hood.

Youthful state is a prime of life filled with exciting exuberances. At this stage of life, youths find themselves at the crossroad and face certain challenging experiences that tend to draw them away from the purpose of God, so all these stages of life need to be handled cautiously. More importantly, parents need to play their roles in child upbring, so that when these children will grow to youthful or adolescent stage, their peer groups will not affect them or influence their character negatively. That brings us to ignorance to secrets life achievements. If parents didn't play their parts or roles very well, the effect following ignorance of secrets of life achievements will affect them. If you fail to plan, then you plan to fail, again ignorance is not an excuse in any development or life achievement, because once a mistake is made, the damage is done. The impact is there to be felt unless there is divine intervention.

Over coming life challenges is determined by how experienced you are and it needs struggle to survive. It needs wisdom and hard work to achieve our life goals. Therefore, if you are unaware or ignorance of how to struggle for life, or you depend on your family members or friends, woe to you, because you will end up becoming a failure or drop out in life. Mistakes of life are one of the results of ignorance of secrets of life achievements. The consequences of loose living by young people lead to frustration in life, joblessness, useless, drop out from schools et-cetera. This also makes them join criminals full of immorality of any kind, drug addiction that may lead to mental or psychiatric illness. Furthermore, some of them will end up joining cult members. Who kill people and sacrifice their relations to make money. At the end of every thing, they will sacrifice themselves. They don't live long to enjoy their wealth. Some of them sacrifice their reproductive organs and will not have any child in life. Oh what a useless life! God forbid. Eventually hell fire is awaiting the person. "What shall it profit a man if he gains the whole world and loses his soul" Luke 9vs25 any mistake in the youthful age is irreversible and regretful later in life. Hence, there is need for caution now on how one lives ones life, and a serious commitment to righteous living. The grace of God is available and capable of sustaining the youth above the powers of the destructive one. Once you hide the word of God in your heart, it will help you not to sin against God "Psalm 119 v 11" there by escaping the consequences following ignorance of secrets of life achievements. Again, when you think you have made it in life during your adult stage or you are opportuned to assume one of the leadership posts, be careful. Don't be self centred. Remember those under you and don't deny any body his/her due promotion. Don't embezzle. Don't use your post to mess up ladies, I mean before giving any body Job. Be transparent in all your dealings with people. Help the poor and the less privileged members of the society. Make the conditions of your workers comfortable. When all these advice are heeded, diligently, you will be the best leader nationally and globally.

Commendation and connections will follow you. You will live a long life. You will be free in life, without security men to follow you around. Both the poor and the rich will be hailing and praying for you and the peace of God will be your portion. Remember that "the love of money is the root of all evils" 1 Tim 6vs 10. And that good name is better than silver and gold. Be a model and leave legacies for your generation.

SUMMARY AND CONCLUSION

The secrets of life achievements in a nut shell wants to expose to you what you ought to know and do so that you will be successful in life. It deals with how you will achieve a lot by knowing the secrets of life achievements and applying them to the challenges of life. Mistakes of life are highly exposed and dealt with in a simplified language. It also explains the goal-setting, long and short goals to achieve your desired purpose in life. Finally, it discloses the consequences as a result of ignorance of the secrets of life achievements. Any mistake made during ones youth or any challenge approached wrongly is irreversible and full of regrets. A stitch in time saves nine. Prevention is better than cure. To be forewarned is to be forearmed. Be diligent and wise, avoiding life threatening characters because good name is better than silver and gold. Look unto Jesus the author and finisher of our faith. He is the perfect God. Trust and obey Him for perpetual enjoyment of his abundant blessings.

RECOMMENDATIONS.

The following recommendations are:

1.	Promotion of child training, beginning from parent at home, in the church under children ministries, and at school. Moral instruction should be given to children every morning devotion or assembly.

2.	Youth seminars and conferences should be conducted for our youths and singles, at least once a month.

3.	Marriage courses/seminars should be organized for married couples, so that there will be no mistakes in life and no broken homes.

REFERENCES

1. Demas, A. (2011). CONQUER YOUR WORLD. Calabar: King view Publishing house.

2. Jane's. (2010), CHALLENGES OF LIFE. Engel: Cecta (Nig) ltd.

3. http://www.mindtools.com/page ohtml personal goal.setting.Retrieved January 20,2010

4. http://www.quotationpage.commistakeR etrieved January 20, 2010.

5. http://www.soul-book.com/life challenges. Retrieved January 19,2010.

6.   Hughes, R. (2010). DVORCE AND CHILDREN. Retrieve January 20,2010 from http://www.@health.com/consumer/disorders/children divoorce.html.

7.   Nworie, R.O.C (2002). SURE WAY TO FAMILY PEACE AND PROGRESS. Enugu: Cecta (Nig) ltd.

8.   Kenyon, E.W. (2010), **SIGN-POST ON THE ROAD TO SUCCESS.** U.S.A; Kenyon's gospel publishing society.

9.   Sally, W. 6th Edition. Oxford Advance Learner's Dictionary. China: Oxford University Press.

10.   THOMAS .N. THE NELSON STUDY BIBLE NEW KING JAMES VERSION. U.S.A: A Division of Thomas Nelson, Inc.